The FJH Young Beginner Guitar Method 1

Includes Free Downloadable Recordings!

PHILIP GROEBER

DAVID HOGE

LEO WELCH

REY SANCHEZ

D1546623

Production: Frank and Gail Hackinson

Production Coordinator: Philip Groeber

Special Editing: John and B.J. Sutherland, Carol Matz

Pilot Editors: Rick Burgess, Georgia; Paul Geller, California; Jaime Guiscafré, Wisconsin; Romana Hartmetz, Virginia; Wanda Iris Rivera-Ferri, Florida; Bob Shaw, Georgia

Cover Design/Illustrations: Terpstra Design, San Francisco

Photography: Lynn Ivory, Master Photographer, Tallahassee

Cover Photo: courtesy of C.F. Martin Guitar & Co., Inc., Nazareth, PA

Engraving: Tempo Music Press, Inc.

Printer: Tempo Music Press, Inc.

THE FJH MUSIC COMPANY INC.

Frank J. Hackinson

ISBN-13: 978-1-56939-165-5

A Note to the Teacher

The FJH Young Beginner Guitar Method is a carefully graded course designed to instruct the modern guitarist to be proficient in solo playing, chord accompaniment, and chord-melody style. Solid musicianship skills are developed by exposing the student to the many styles typically encountered in today's musical world. The series consists of five books for each level: Lesson, Theory Activity, Performance, Exploring Chords, and Christmas. The Lesson Book, Theory Activity Book, and Performance Book are carefully correlated to one another. The Exploring Chords and Christmas Books may be used according to the needs of the individual student.

The FJH Young Beginner Lesson Book 1 includes the following features:

- A pre-reading section allows the student to play songs by reading fret numbers only.

- The student learns basic notes (natural notes in first position on strings one, two, and three) and rhythms (whole, dotted half, half, and quarter notes), making the *Young Beginner* an ideal starting point for elementary guitarists of all ages.

- This book is equally adaptable to pick-style or classical technique.

- The songs and pieces in this book are suitable for public performance. Optional teacher duets (with chord names) offer a variety of accompaniment styles.

- Dynamics are introduced to develop musicianship at an early level.

Other features:

 Enables the student to learn correct technical skills from the very first lesson.

 Offers important information relating to the music and presents historical facts.

 Provides new concepts for performance that stimulate creativity.

Some Helpful Hints

- The student should frequently review the material presented in "Guitar Basics," pages 4–11.

- A steady beat (pulse) is required to establish basic rhythm skills. The use of a metronome is encouraged. Suggested tempi are given.

- Referring to the "Note Review Chart" will reinforce note-reading skills.

- The student should be thoroughly familiar with his or her part before the teacher duet part is used, giving special attention to accurate rhythm.

A Certificate of Achievement is available as a free download on our website.

Notes to the Student

- Practice at your own pace. Move ahead when you feel comfortable playing the music you have just learned.

- Move on to the next lesson only after having completed the correlating lesson material in the other books in the series. Corresponding page numbers can be found in the margins.

Contents

Guitar Basics

TYPES OF GUITARS

Acoustic Guitar

The acoustic guitar has steel strings and a bright, ringing tone. Pick-style and finger-style playing are both common on the acoustic guitar.

Electric Guitar

The electric guitar is used for music that requires a wide range of volume and tone. The most common types have a solid body. Pick-style is more common, but finger-style playing is also used. When practicing on the electric guitar, always use an amplifier.

Classical Guitar

The classical guitar has nylon strings which are easier to press down than the steel strings found on an acoustic guitar. The fingerboard and string spacing is wide, which makes finding the strings easier for both hands. Finger-style is the most common type of music played on the classical guitar.

Learning to play guitar is much easier with a quality instrument. Is your guitar:

- the right size for you? (full, three-quarter, or half)
- equipped with new strings?
- in good playing condition? Are the strings easy to press down?

HOLDING THE GUITAR

Sitting with the guitar

The guitar should rest comfortably on your lap. The neck of the guitar should be raised slightly and does not need to be supported by the left arm. The right leg may be crossed over the left leg for added support.

Standing

A guitar strap is used to hold the guitar in correct playing position. Try standing with your guitar only after becoming very comfortable with a sitting position.

Classical position

The left leg is raised by a footstand which places the guitar in a very secure position.

Your teacher can help you decide which position is best for you. In *all* of the positions above:

- The shoulders are relaxed and the back is straight.
- The hands are not actually used to hold the guitar, but are free to play.
- The neck of the guitar is slanted upward.

THE RIGHT HAND; USING THE PICK

The **pick** (flat-pick or plectrum) is used to strum the strings.
Some students may choose to use the right-hand thumb or fingers
instead of a pick. If using a pick, start with a tear-drop shape
of medium thickness.

**Holding the pick in a relaxed and secure way is important
in learning to play accurately, build speed, and produce
a good sound.**

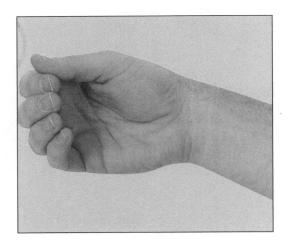

Imagine you are holding an egg in
your right hand.

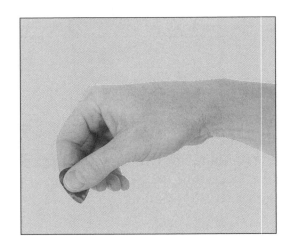

With your right-hand fingers gently
curved, hold the pick lightly between
your thumb and index finger.

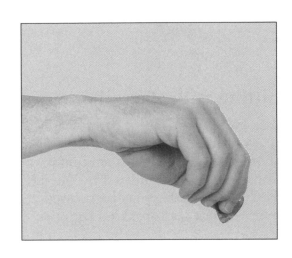

The fingers remain in a relaxed,
tucked position while playing.

PLAYING DOWNSTROKES AND UPSTROKES

The strings may be sounded by using **downstrokes** (⊓) or **upstrokes** (V) with the guitar pick.

To play a **downstroke** (⊓), strum the string(s) using a downward sweeping motion with the pick.

To play an **upstroke** (V), strum the string(s) using an upward sweeping motion with the pick.

Play the following exercise slowly, strumming *all six strings* each time.

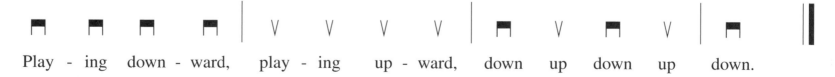

POWER PLAY Downstrokes and upstrokes also may be used on single strings.
Practice the pattern ⊓ V ⊓ V on each of the six guitar strings.
How many times can you play the pattern without missing the string?

POSITIONING THE LEFT HAND

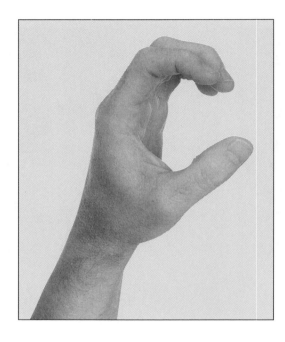

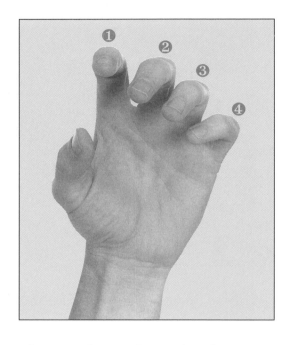

Begin with your left arm hanging relaxed by your side. Next, bend your arm at the elbow as you move your hand toward the guitar neck. Your left shoulder should remain relaxed at all times.

Make a "C" shape with your left thumb and fingers, while keeping your wrist relaxed and slightly bent. Your fingers should be curved gently, as if you were holding a bubble.

The roundness of your hand position helps to make the different length fingers feel the same while you play the guitar. The fingers are numbered as shown: first ❶, second ❷, third ❸, and fourth ❹.

TECHNIQUE TIP

Playing with the left hand in the proper position (as shown above), will make it easier for you to press the strings down with the tips of your fingers.

PRESSING DOWN THE STRINGS

correct

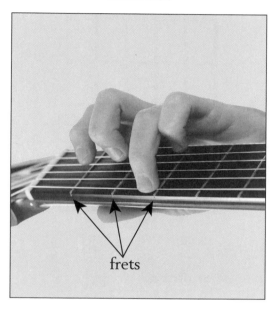

frets

incorrect

thumb position

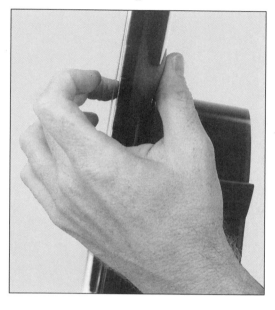

Press with the fingertip directly *behind* the fret. Use just enough pressure to produce a clear sound. For best results, the left-hand fingernails should be kept short.

The above picture shows a common problem: the finger is not close enough to the fret, and is applying too much pressure. This finger position can cause the string to buzz.

The thumb should touch lightly on the back of the guitar neck opposite the fingertips. It remains in a natural position. The palm does not touch the back of the neck.

POWER PLAY

Using any left-hand finger, play on different strings and frets. Try to make a clear, clean sound. When you play notes on the higher-numbered frets, the sound (pitch) of the notes also becomes higher.

PARTS OF THE GUITAR

THE FINGERBOARD DIAGRAM

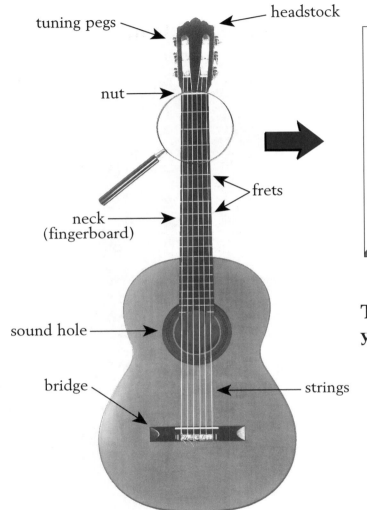

Close-up of the fingerboard

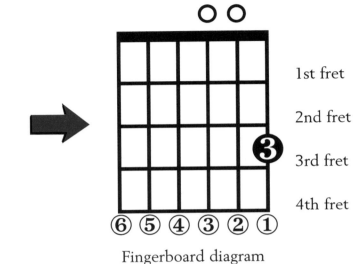

Fingerboard diagram

The purpose of the fingerboard diagram is to show you where to play each note.

- Numbers in circles (① ② etc.) show the string numbers.
- Dots (❸) will show you where to place your left-hand fingers.
- A circle (○) means an open string; no left-hand fingers are used.
- In the example above, use your third finger to play the first string at the third fret. The second and third strings are played open.

You may think that the strings *closest to the floor* (while holding the guitar) are the lower strings…but just the opposite is true! **The strings closest to the floor are actually the higher strings** because they are higher in pitch (sound).

THREE WAYS TO TUNE THE GUITAR

1. Using an electronic tuner

The *easiest* way to tune your guitar is with an **electronic tuner**, which comes with simple instructions. Electronic tuners are used by many professional guitarists as well as beginning students. Tuners that clip onto the headstock make tuning the guitar a little easier.

2. Tuning to a keyboard

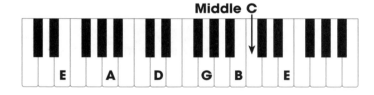

Your guitar can be tuned to a **piano**, an **organ**, or an **electronic keyboard**. Important: Notice the location of Middle C on the chart above.

3. Tuning the guitar to itself

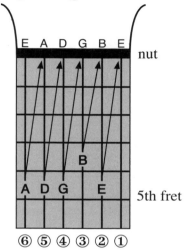

You also may tune the guitar to itself. This is called **relative tuning**. See the chart below.

Assuming that string ⑥ is correctly tuned to E:			
PRESS	STRING	TO GET THE PITCH	TO TUNE OPEN STRING
the 5th fret of	⑥	A	⑤
the 5th fret of	⑤	D	④
the 5th fret of	④	G	③
the 4th fret of	③	B	②
the 5th fret of	②	E	①

TECHNIQUE TIP It is very important that your guitar be tuned correctly each time you practice. Because learning to tune by ear is a skill which takes time to develop, an electronic tuner is a worthwhile investment. If your guitar is always tuned correctly, you will gradually develop the skill to tune by ear.

Making Music

USING FRET NUMBERS TO PLAY MUSIC ON THE FIRST STRING

- The piece below is played on the first (thinnest) string.
- **The 0 means an open string.** No left-hand fingers will be used in *Olympic Bronze*.

Play the open first string using downstrokes (⊓). Play slowly and evenly, *one note per second.*
Your right hand will be playing downstrokes throughout this book.

Student solo on the first string

Olympic Bronze

 A metronome is a small machine or an inexpensive app used to help keep a steady beat. When set to ♩ = **60**, the metronome clicks or beeps sixty times per minute, or one time every second.

Tracks
3   6•7

Melody (in notation)

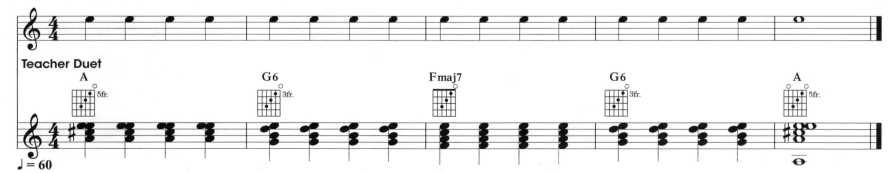

Teacher Duet

♩ = 60

- Using *any left-hand finger,* press down the first string at the fifth fret (**5**).

Olympic Silver

etc.

5 5 5 5 | 5 5 5 5 | 5 5 5 5 | 5 5 5 5 | 5

- The piece below uses notes on the fifth fret (**5**) as well as the open string (**0**).

- **The fives (5) are placed higher than the zeros (0) because the 5 is a higher pitch.**

Olympic Gold

etc.

5 5 5 5 | 0 0 0 0 | 5 5 0 0 | 5 0 5 0 | 5

Melody (in notation) for *Olympic Silver* combined with *Olympic Gold*

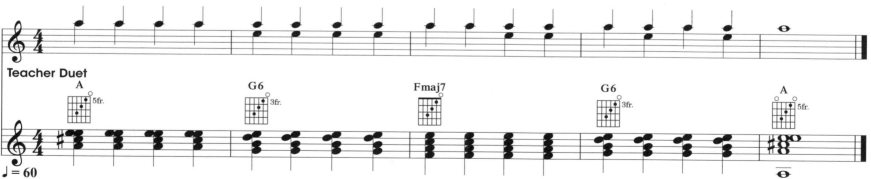

This duet part is to be played for both *Olympic Silver* and *Olympic Gold.*

Note to the teacher: Allow students to choose which left-hand fingers they use.
Position playing is introduced along with note reading.

PLAYING FAMILIAR SONGS USING FRET NUMBERS

Rain, Rain, Go Away is also played on the first string.
- Three notes are used: the open string (**0**); the third fret (**3**); and the fifth fret (**5**).
- Use any left-hand finger to press the string down. If one finger gets tired, use another.
- Play downstrokes with your guitar pick or thumb.

Rain, Rain, Go Away

Traditional

Practice singing the words to *Rain, Rain, Go Away* as you play the notes. You will have mastered this song when you can play as easily as you sing.

- *Hot Cross Buns* is played on the first string and uses frets **3**, **5**, and **7**.
- Use any left-hand finger for each note, remembering to play with your fingertips.
- No open strings will be used in this song.

Hot Cross Buns

Traditional

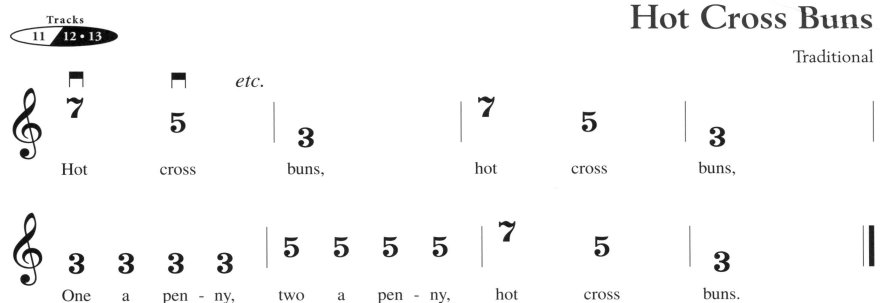

etc.

| 7 | 5 | 3 | | 7 | 5 | 3 | |
| Hot | cross | buns, | | hot | cross | buns, | |

| 3 3 3 3 | 5 5 5 5 | 7 | 5 | 3 | |
| One a pen - ny, | two a pen - ny, | hot | cross | buns. | |

TECHNIQUE TIP

When a finger moves from one note to another on the same string, the left-hand fingertip should continue to gently touch the string. This technique is called using a **guide finger**. Using guide fingers will help you move easily from one note to another.

Melody (in notation)

Teacher Duet

- *A Melody from Mozart* is played on the first string and uses frets **0**, **2**, **4**, **5**, **7**, and **9**.
- Play slowly and evenly with a nice, full sound.
- Use any left-hand finger to press the string down.

A Melody from Mozart
Twinkle, Twinkle Little Star

Traditional

etc.

0 0   7   7 | 9 9 7 | 5 5 4 4 | 2 2 0

Twin - kle, twin - kle   lit - tle   star,   how   I   won - der   what you are!

Your left hand should be ready to play the seventh fret (**7**) before you start playing the open string (**0**) at the beginning of the song.

Tracks
14 / 16 • 17

This familiar melody was used by Wolfgang Amadeus Mozart (MŌ TZART), (1756–1791), in a composition written for the piano.

Melody (in notation)

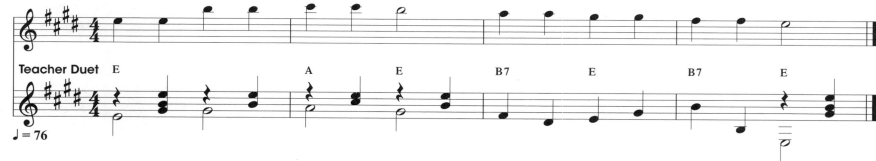

Teacher Duet   E   A   E   B7   E   B7   E

♩ = 76

Now learn the rest of the melody.

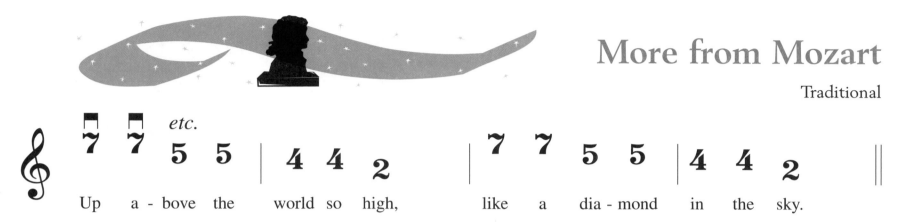

More from Mozart

Traditional

etc.

7 7 5 5 | 4 4 2 | 7 7 5 5 | 4 4 2 ||

Up a - bove the world so high, like a dia - mond in the sky.

If you want to play all of *Twinkle, Twinkle Little Star*, play page 16 first, then page 17. Then, go back to play page 16 again for the ending.

Tracks
15 / 16 • 17

Melody (in notation)

repeat page 16

Teacher Duet

♩ = 76

Congratulations!

You have completed the section on learning to play music using fret numbers.

You are now ready to learn how to read music! ➡

2 Notes on the First String

Music Terms

- The **staff** is a precise way of showing high and low notes.
- It has five lines and four spaces on which notes are written.

- The names of notes come from the music alphabet: A, B, C, D, E, F, and G.
- Notes written higher on the staff are for higher pitches. Notes written lower on the staff are for lower pitches.

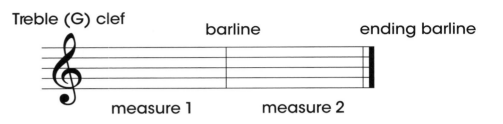

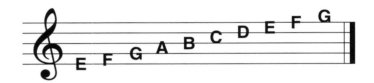

The following can help you remember the names of the line and space notes on the staff.

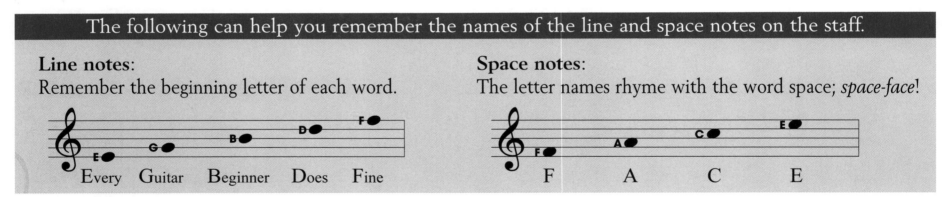

Line notes:
Remember the beginning letter of each word.

Every Guitar Beginner Does Fine

Space notes:
The letter names rhyme with the word space; *space-face*!

F   A   C   E

THE QUARTER NOTE

- The quarter note gets one beat. ♩ = 1 beat
- When playing quarter notes, keep a steady beat.

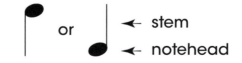

For the following exercise, your teacher will tap a steady beat or you may use a metronome. Play quarter notes, playing the open first string on every tap or click. Practice at slow and fast tempos (speeds).

NEW NOTE E

 E

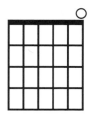

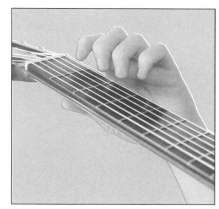

The E note is located in the top space of the staff.

To play E, simply play the open first string.

The Spanish Bullfight

Count aloud with a steady beat.

Count evenly: 1   2   3   4   1   2   3   4   1   2   3   4   1   2   3   4

MUSIC MASTER

Spanish classical guitarist Andrés Segovia (1893–1987) is considered by many to be the greatest guitarist of all time. The guitar is the national instrument of Spain.

Tracks
18 / 19 • 20

Teacher Duet

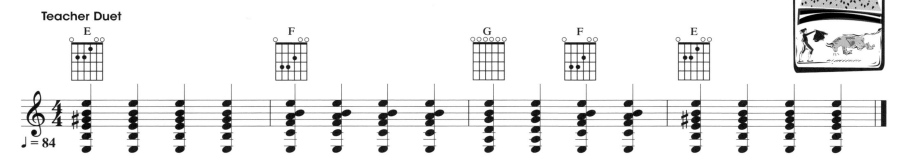

E   F   G   F   E

♩ = 84

Note to the teacher: *The Spanish Bullfight* uses specialized chords for F and G, intended for this page only. These chord names only approximate the harmony.

NEW NOTE F

F

The F note is located on the top line of the staff.

To play F, place your first finger ❶ on the first string at the first fret.

Same Note Blues

Count evenly: 1 2 3 4 1 2 3 4 1 2 3 4 1 2 3 4

Tracks
21 / 22 • 23

Keep a steady beat when playing quarter notes.

Use only the tip of the finger, and play just behind the fret as shown in the photographs above.

Teacher Duet

Swing rhythm (♫ = ♩³♪)

F7   B♭7   C7   B♭7   F7

♩ = 72

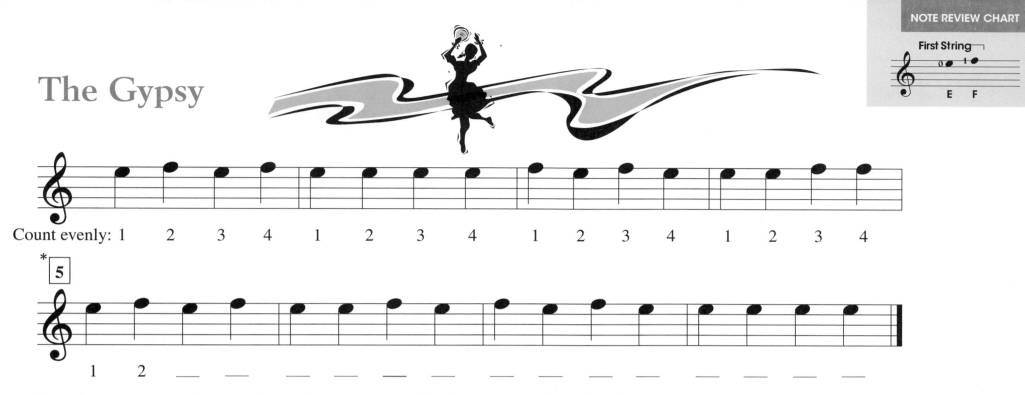

The Gypsy

First String

E F

Count evenly: 1 2 3 4 1 2 3 4 1 2 3 4 1 2 3 4

*5

1 2 — — — — — — — — — — — —

Finish writing in the numbers for counting. Each measure has four beats.

Tracks
24 / 25 • 26

When you are playing the open E notes, keep the tip of your
first finger close to the string, ready to play the F notes.

Teacher Duet

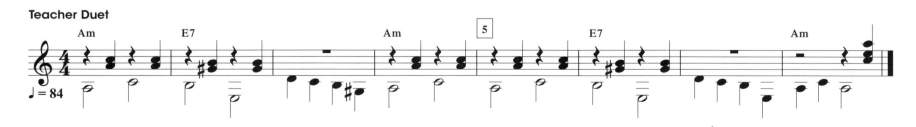

*This is a measure number; it helps musicians easily find any measure of music.

016

21

NEW NOTE G

The G note is located just above the top line of the staff.

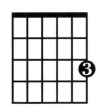

To play G, place your third finger ❸ on the first string at the third fret.

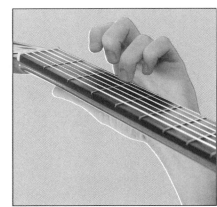

Tracks 27 / 28 • 29

Solid Rock

Teacher Duet

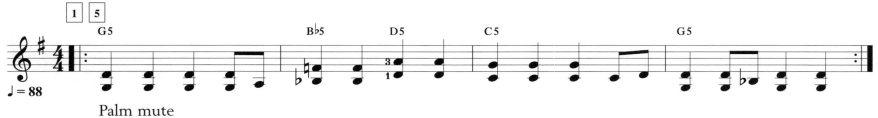

Palm mute

At the Malt Shop

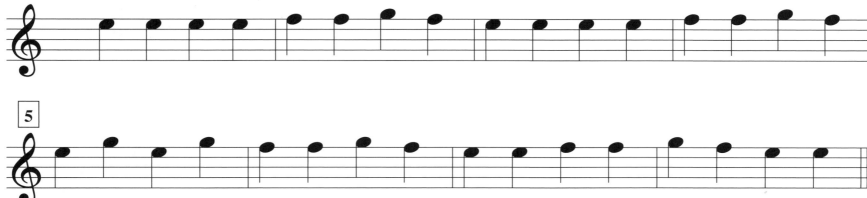

When playing the G notes, remember to place your third finger *behind* the third fret in order to produce a clear sound.

Teacher Duet

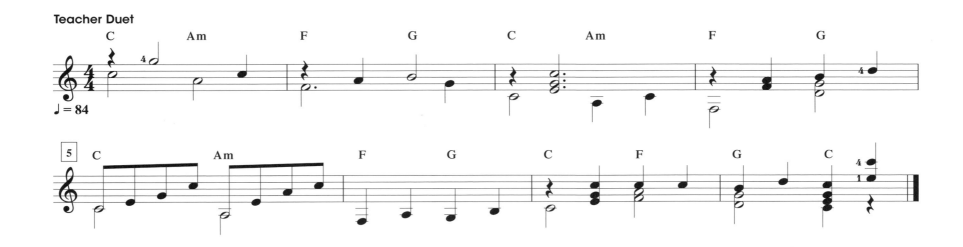

3 Beginning Rhythm

$\frac{4}{4}$ TIME SIGNATURE

The two numbers placed after the treble clef are called the **time signature**.

- The top number tells us how many beats are in a measure.
- The bottom number tells us what kind of note gets one beat.

The $\frac{4}{4}$ (four-four) time signature means:

4 = four beats per measure; and

4 = the quarter note gets one beat

    (the number 4 at the bottom means the quarter note ♩).

Finish writing the numbers for counting beats on the blank lines below the staff.
Then count aloud with a steady beat as you play.

time signature

count: 1   2   3   4   ___ ___ ___ ___ ___ ___ ___ ___ ___ ___ ___ ___

Go back to pages 19–23 and write in the missing $\frac{4}{4}$ time signatures
at the beginning of each piece.

First String

E   F   G

THE HALF NOTE

The half note gets two beats. 𝅗𝅥 = 2 beats
How does the half note look different from the quarter note?

𝅗𝅥 or 𝅗𝅥

Getting Ready for Half Notes

- Count aloud "**1 2, 1 2**" several times, evenly.
- Get ready to play the open first string E. While saying "**1 2,**" play E when you say "**1.**"
- Now say "**3 4, 3 4**" several times, evenly. Play E only when you say "**3.**"
- While counting "**1 2 3 4,**" play E when you say "**1**" and "**3.**"

Play the following half notes using E, F, and G.
Teacher and student play together while the student counts aloud.

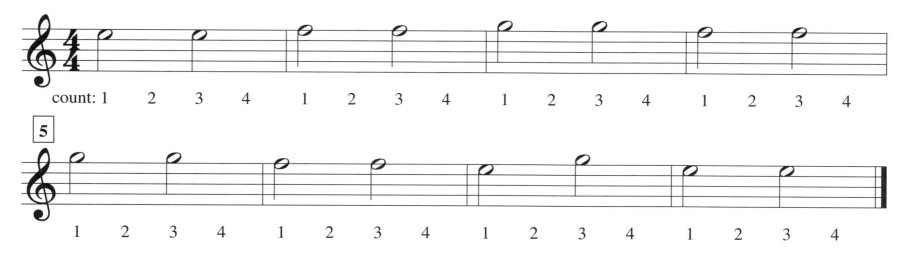

count: 1   2   3   4   1   2   3   4   1   2   3   4   1   2   3   4

5

1   2   3   4   1   2   3   4   1   2   3   4   1   2   3   4

POWER PLAY

For the following exercise, your teacher will tap a steady beat or you may use a metronome. Play quarter notes using the open first string E. When instructed, change to half notes. Follow your teacher's directions, playing quarter notes or half notes.

Tracks
33 / 34 • 35

Over Distant Mountains

RHYTHM REMINDER: *Over Distant Mountains* uses both quarter notes and half notes.

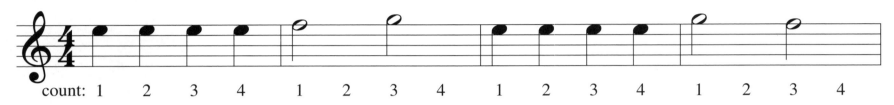

count: 1 2 3 4   1 2 3 4   1 2 3 4   1 2 3 4

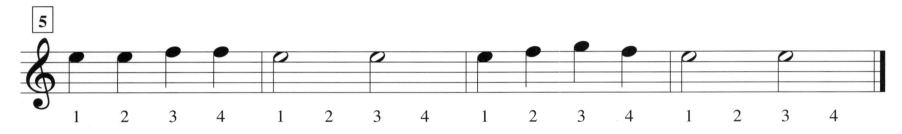

1 2 3 4   1 2 3 4   1 2 3 4   1 2 3 4

Say the names of the notes as you play them.

Teacher Duet

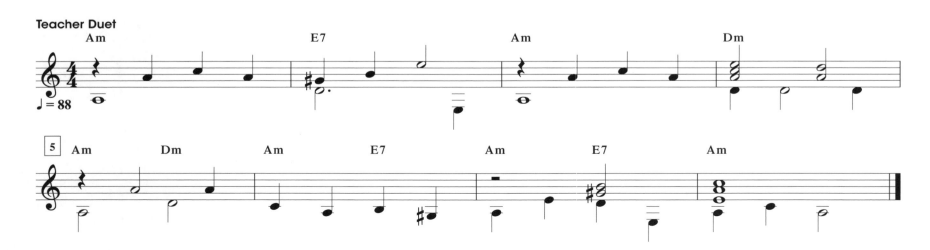

26

G1

There and Back Again

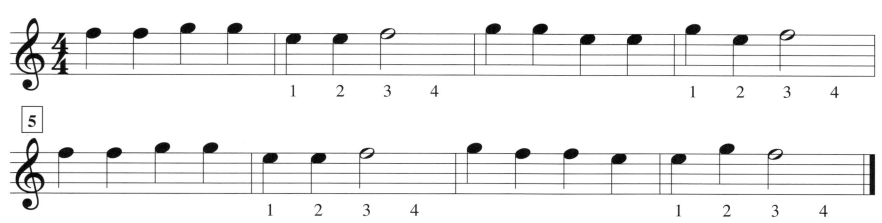

MUSIC MASTER

There and Back Again contains half notes that start on beat three.
Be sure you allow each half note to sound for two full beats (beats three *and* four).
Count aloud. Counting numbers are provided for measures with new rhythms.

Tracks
36 / 37 • 38

Teacher Duet

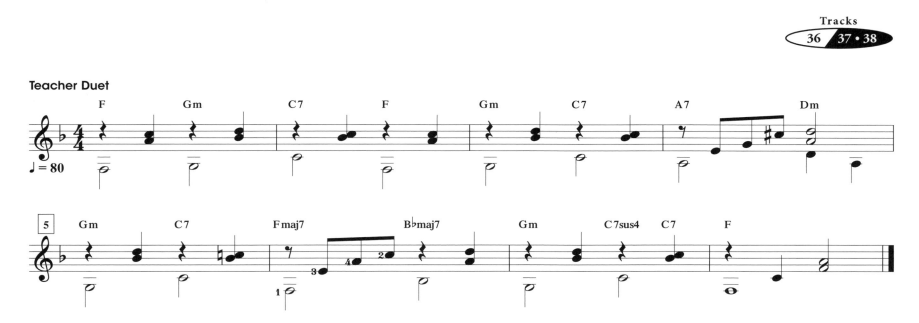

NEW NOTE D

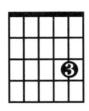

The D note is located on the fourth line of the staff.

To play D, place your third finger ❸ on the second string at the third fret.

Tracks
39 / 40 • 41

Egyptian Festival

```
1   2   3   4   1   2   3   4
```

Teacher Duet

♩ = 112

G10

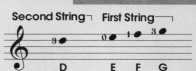
NOTE REVIEW CHART

Tale of the Troubadour

POWER PLAY

Moving from one string to another will become easy with practice.
Repeat the example below several times, playing slowly and evenly.
Do not attempt to play fast until you can play the example well at a slow tempo (speed).

Tracks 42 / 43 · 44

Teacher Duet

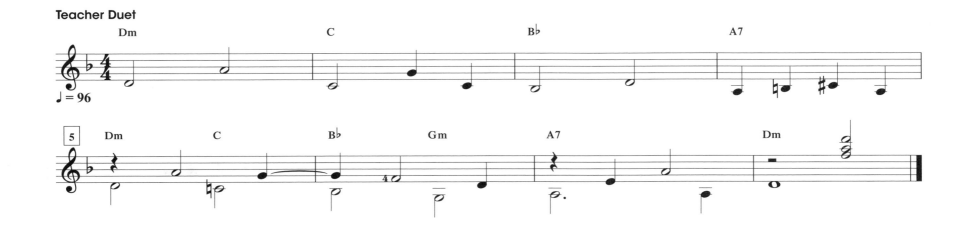

NEW NOTE C

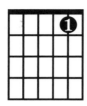

The C note is located in the third space of the staff.

To play C, place your first finger ❶ on the second string at the first fret.

A Little Jazz

Teacher Duet

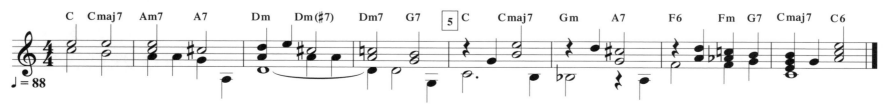

Caribbean Breeze

Tracks
48 / 49 • 50

TECHNIQUE TIP Allow each note to sound as long as possible. This technique (**legato**) will help you to play smoothly by connecting the notes to each other.

Teacher Duet

NEW NOTE B

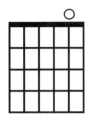

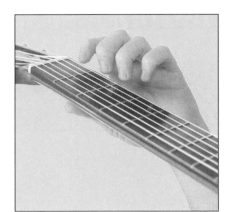

The B note is located on the third (middle) line of the staff.

To play B, simply play the open second string.

Flamenco Dancer

1   2   3   4   1   2   3   4

5

MUSIC MASTER

Flamenco is a type of Spanish folk music that uses the guitar to accompany singers and dancers.

Tracks 51 / 52 • 53

Teacher Duet

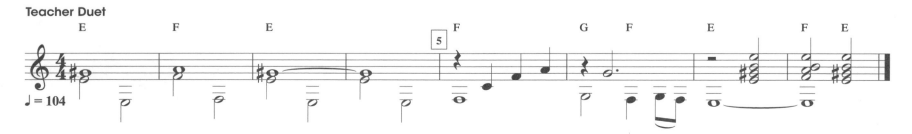

E   F   E   F   G   F   E   F   E

♩ = 104

32

G10

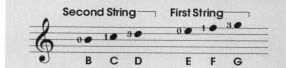

Estudio
Study

Matteo Carcassi
(1792–1853)
(arranged)

Tracks
54 · 55 · 56

Matteo Carcassi was a famous Italian classical guitarist.
The melody and the teacher duet of *Estudio* were
originally written to be played on one guitar.

Teacher Duet

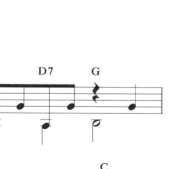

16

5 Notes on the Third String

NEW NOTE A

The A note is located in the second space of the staff.

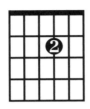

To play A, place the second finger ❷ on the third string at the second fret.

March of the Animals

Notes that are placed below the middle line of the staff have stems that point up. New note A is the first note you have learned with an *upstem*.

Tracks
57 / 58 • 59

Teacher Duet

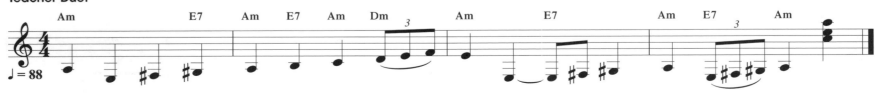

♩ = 88

A Winter's Journey

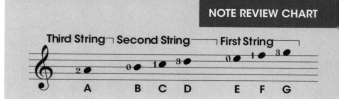

Tracks
60 / 61 • 62

In measures one and three, you may hold the A note with your second finger ❷ *for the entire measure* while you play the open first string E.

Teacher Duet

NEW NOTE G

The G note is located on the second line of the staff.

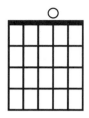

To play G, simply play the open third string.

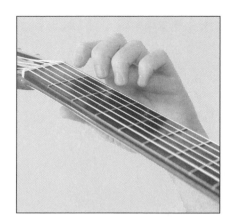

Au Clair de la Lune
By the Light of the Moon

French Folk Song

Tracks 63 / 64 • 65

5

Teacher Duet

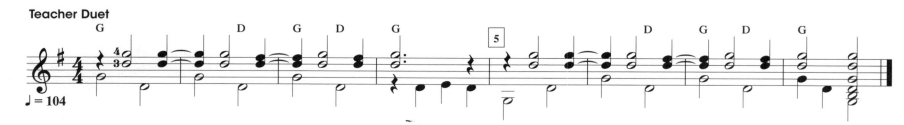

♩ = 104

36

Mustang Canyon

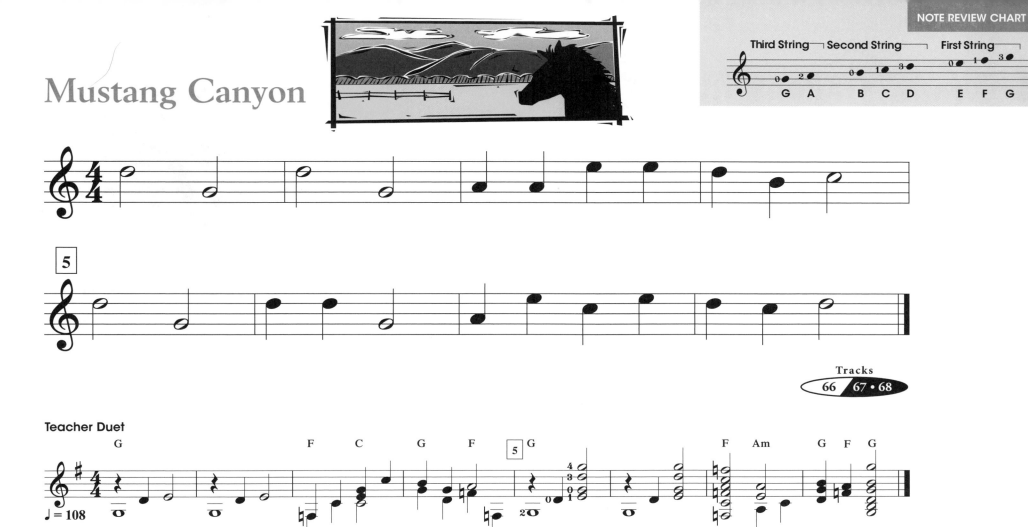

Tracks
66 / 67 • 68

Teacher Duet

♩ = 108

You now know two different G notes. They are an **octave** (eight notes) apart.
Practice going back and forth between the two G notes.
Play the example below several times without stopping.

Fast

1 2 3 4   1 2 3 4   1 2 3 4   1 2 3 4

6 More On Rhythm

THE WHOLE NOTE

- The whole note gets four beats. **o** = 4 beats
- Four even counts must take place before you play the next note.
- Count "**1 2 3 4**" for each whole note.

Always keep an even, steady beat.

Pachelbel Canon

Johann Pachelbel
(1653–1706)

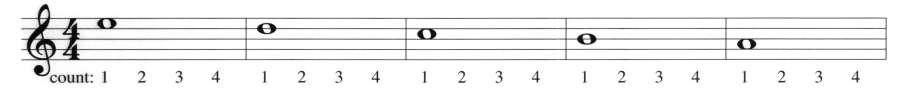

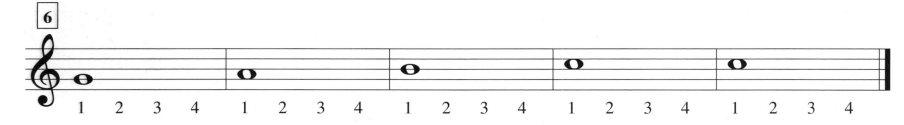

RHYTHM REMINDER: When playing in 4/4 time, whole notes will always
be played on the first beat of the measure.

Tracks
69 / 70 • 71

Teacher Duet

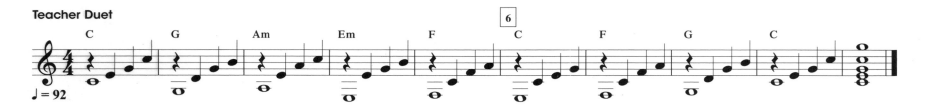

38

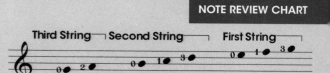

The Emperor's Fanfare

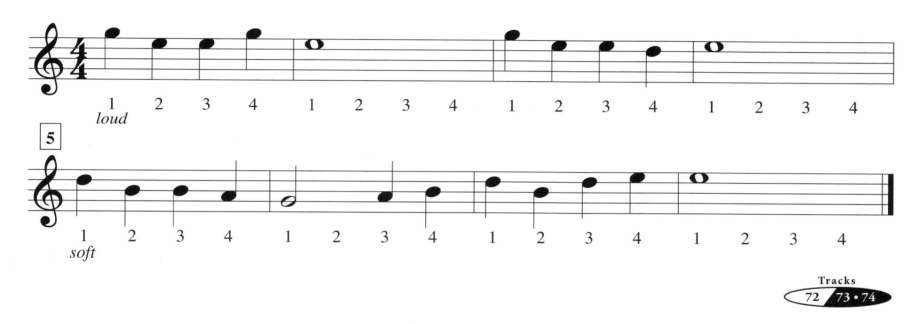

Tracks
72 / 73 • 74

MUSIC MASTER Music may use words or symbols called **dynamics** to tell the performer how loudly or softly to play. *Exaggerating* the dynamics adds expression to your music.

Teacher Duet

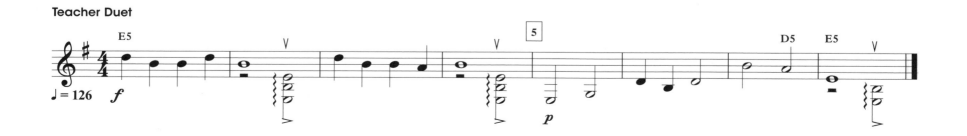

Arrorró Mi Niño
Lullaby, My Baby
Argentinean Folk Song

A - rro - rró mi ni - ño, A - rro - rró mi sol,
Lul - la - by, my ba - by, Lul - la - by, my son,

5

A - rro - rró pe - da - zo, de mi cor - a - zón.
Lul - la - by, my sweet - heart, Moth - er's lit - tle one.

Tracks
75 / 76 • 77

POWER PLAY

A lullaby is a soft and gentle song used to lull a child to sleep.
Be sure to play *Arrorró Mi Niño* softly.

Teacher Duet

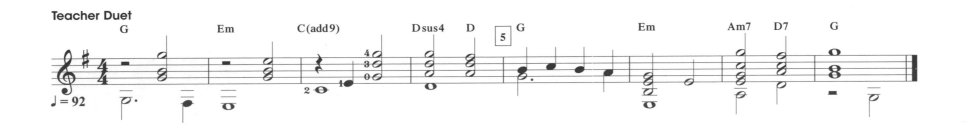

40

Appalachian Dulcimer

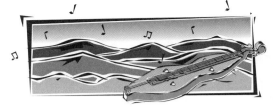
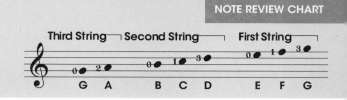

Tracks 78 79 • 80

 The dulcimer used in Appalachian music is a small, wooden, three-stringed instrument with frets. It is often used to accompany singers. Play near the bridge to make a bright sound like a dulcimer.

Teacher Duet

♩ = 104   Let notes ring

16

41

7 ¾ Time Signature

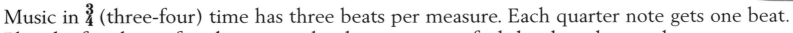

3 = three beats per measure
4 = the quarter note gets one beat

Music in ¾ (three-four) time has three beats per measure. Each quarter note gets one beat.
Play the first beat of each measure louder so you can feel the three-beat pulse.
Count two measures of ¾ before you begin.

*Folias de España**

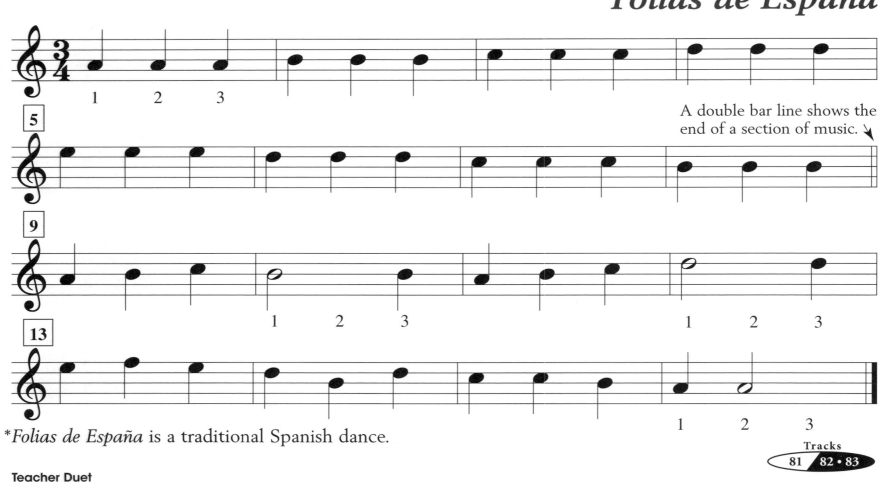

A double bar line shows the
end of a section of music.

Folias de España is a traditional Spanish dance.

Tracks
81 82 • 83

Teacher Duet

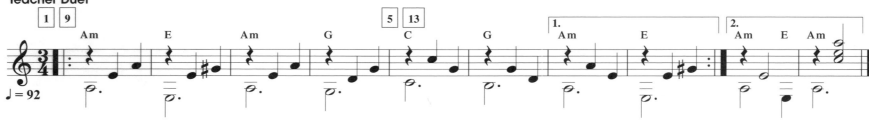

42

G

THE DOTTED HALF NOTE

A dotted half note gets three beats. $\bullet$ = 3 beats

Classical Waltz

Mauro Giuliani
(1781–1829)
(arranged)

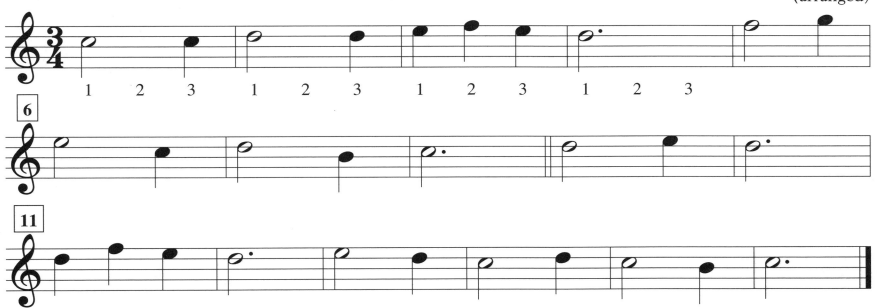

MUSIC MASTER

A waltz is a dance that has three beats per measure.
It was very popular in Europe during the 1800s.

Tracks
84 / 85 • 86

16

8 Putting It All Together

Ode to Joy
(from the Ninth Symphony)

Ludwig van Beethoven
(1770–1827)

medium loud

Tracks
87 / 88 • 89

Teacher Duet

♩ = 108 *mp*

9

soft

13

loud

MUSIC MASTER

Ludwig van Beethoven is considered to be one of the greatest composers in all of music history. *Ode to Joy* is one of his best-known melodies.

Celtic Jig

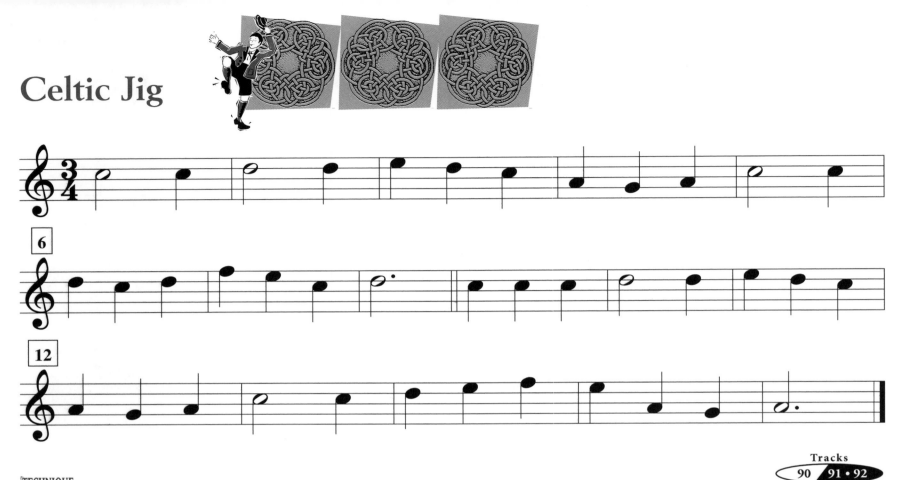

Tracks
90 / 91 • 92

TECHNIQUE TIP You may hold down your first finger in measures five and six while you are playing the D notes on the third fret.

Teacher Duet

46

Glossary

SIGN	TERM	DEFINITION
❶❷❸❹		Left-hand finger numbers.
⑥⑤④③②①		String numbers.
𝅗𝅥.	dotted half note	Hold this note for three beats.
	dynamics	Symbols or words that indicate how loud or soft to play.
	first position	The first finger ❶ of the left hand plays notes on the first fret; the second finger ❷, the second fret; the third finger ❸, the third fret; and the fourth finger ❹, the fourth fret.
𝅗𝅥	half note	Hold this note for two beats.
	legato	Smooth and connected with no separation between notes.
	pitch	Pitch is a high or low sound, shown by a note drawn on the staff.
♩	quarter note	Hold this note for one beat.
	rhythm	Note values (♩, 𝅗𝅥, 𝅗𝅥., 𝅝) which indicate how long to hold each note.
$\frac{4}{4}$	time signature	(*four-four*) Four beats per measure. The ♩ gets one beat.
$\frac{3}{4}$	time signature	(*three-four*) Three beats per measure. The ♩ gets one beat.
𝅝	whole note	Hold this note for four beats.

The FJH Young Beginner Guitar Method and Supplemental Material

The FJH Young Beginner Guitar Method is a well-conceived, graded guitar method designed especially for the younger beginner. Presenting one concept at a time, the method engages students with lively songs instead of exercises. Both teacher and student will enjoy the music right from the beginning! Adaptable in pick style or classical technique.

There are five publications in each of the three levels:
Lesson, Theory-Activity, Performance, Exploring Chords, and Christmas.

Level 1
Includes a pre-reading section that allows the student to play songs by reading fret numbers only. Natural notes in first position on strings one, two, and three are presented, along with basic rhythms. Dynamics are also introduced to develop musicianship at an early level. Includes optional teacher duets with chord names. Rhythmic accuracy is stressed throughout the method.

Level 2
Chords are introduced along with the natural notes on strings four, five, and six. New concepts include eighth notes, chromatics (sharps, flats and naturals), pick-up notes, ties, and rests. Students are encouraged to strum chords to accompany the melody whenever possible. Many optional teacher duets are included. (Students may enjoy playing the teacher duet parts as well!)

Level 3
In Lesson Book 3 the students learn complete chords with many opportunities to strum while the teacher plays the melody. New concepts include: dotted quarter notes, hammer-ons and pull-offs, major and minor pentatonic scales, major key theory and major scales, power chords, palm mute, solo styles, and music in Second Position. Music styles include popular, rock 'n' roll, blues, classics, multi-cultural, and music from various eras.

After the completion of Young Beginner Level 3 students move into **Everybody's Guitar Method**: **G1025 Book 1** if a review is needed; **G1030 Book 2** is the usual choice; **G1048** combines both Books 1 and 2 using tablature.

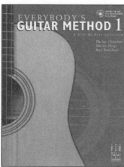

G1025

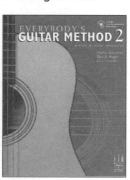

G1030

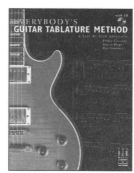

G1048

Supplemental Material for The FJH Young Beginner Guitar Method

GuitarTime Series Christmas
G1001 Primer Level Pick Style
G1002 Level 1 Pick Style
G1003 Level 2 Pick Style
G1004 Level 3 Pick Style
G1005 Level 1 Classical Style
G1006 Level 2 Classical Style

GuitarTime Series Popular Folk
G1007 Primer Level Pick Style
G1008 Level 1 Pick Style
G1009 Level 2 Pick Style
G1010 Level 3 Pick Style
G1011 Level 1 Classical Style
G1012 Level 2 Classical Style

Everybody's Series
G1026 Flash Cards
G1029 Basic Guitar Chords
G1032 Basic Guitar Scales
G1042 Strum & Play Guitar Chords
G1043 Guitar Ensembles
G1049 Ukulele Method 1
G1062 Electric Bass Method 1

Other Publications
G1058 My First Easy To Play Guitar TAB Book
G1060 My First Easy To Play Guitar Scale Book
G1061 My First Easy To Play Guitar Chord Book
G1059 The Big & Easy Songbook for Guitar with Tablature

Visit The FJH Guitar Website: www.fjhmusic.com/guitar
- New Releases
- Information on Every Series
- Online Guitar Tuner
- Online Guitar Chord Generator
- National Federation of Music Clubs FJH Selected Titles
- FJH Guitar Correlation Chart